For Anyone Who's Ever Loved a Dog
This Is the Message They Want You to Know

I KNOW WHY
DOG IS GOD
SPELLED
BACKWARDS

Bob & Cody Wolff

Published by

The Creative Syndicate

10400 Overland Road, Suite 143

Boise, Idaho, USA 83709

Copyediting by Lynette M. Smith

Book Interior Design by Betty Abrantes

Cody Photography by Robert Wolff.
Copyright and all rights reserved.

Book Information:

http://BobAndCody.com

http://CodyAndBob.com

http://RobertWolff.com and

http://amazon.com/author/robertwolff

Print edition ISBN: 978-1-937939-27-4

MOBI electronic edition ISBN: 978-1-937939-28-1

EPUB electronic edition ISBN: 978-1-937939-29-8

First printing 2014

Library of Congress Control Number: 2013902365

Contents

A Little Note From Your Two- and Four-Legged Friends

This book is written for you.

While our names are on the title as authors (Bob, the people buddy, and Cody, the dog buddy), don't let that fool you.

We're just the translators and messengers who simply have one job to do: Give you the message that your Friend, the Best Friend in all the world you will ever know, wants you to read and let sink into your heart.

So smile.

The Best Friend you have ever known will always be the Best Friend you will ever have.

Now.

And forever.

Foreword

We live in an amazing Universe.

Sometimes things happen in our lives where we have no idea of just how that experience will change our lives from that moment on.

Like having a dog.

They give us love.

We give them love.

And they make us better just because we loved them.

But there's more.

Lots more.

Behind the outward affection and love we share with them, come lessons about love, about life and about ourselves that would not and could not have happened unless our dog was in our life.

Yet there's a surprise.

It's a message your most beloved best friend wants you to know, a message you may never have realized.

It's the way *you* changed *your best friend's* life.

You see, you and your dog didn't come into each other's lives by accident.

Oh no. It's much bigger than that.

It was on *purpose*.

You *both* chose *each* other.

Now, you're about to understand why.

Introduction

The day you saw me and I saw you for the first time, is the day both of our lives changed forever.

No one could tell you and me why or how, but on that day, we made the most powerful connection and a bond where we just "knew," deep down inside our heart and soul, we were meant to be together for the rest of our lives.

It is a love, a trust, a companionship, and the most special of all relationships, that nothing or no one will ever have the power to change or to break.

Ours is a love and bond that will last for the rest of this life and in all of the lives in the future that we are going to live together as best friends and soul mates.

Our time together now is only the beginning of the love we will be feeling and sharing for each other in the time to come.

It is a love like we have never felt before, and we will never feel the same love for anyone or anything else, because our love for each other is only "ours."

Just you and me.

Together.

Always close and never wanting to leave and be without each other.

This I promise you.

Best friends.

Soul mates.

Now.

And forever.

I love you.

"Patience"

The day you brought me home is the day my life changed forever.

They say we dogs are the most patient animals in the world, and we can teach our human best friends the meaning of patience, but don't believe them.

I know what it's like to be impatient too.

I know what it's like to be so impatient just knowing whenever you must leave me so you can do the things you must do each day in your life, and how much I don't want you to go.

I know how it feels to see you go and then think about how soon you'll be coming back home to be with me, and how excited and anxious I am going to be to see and hear you walk in the door.

I know how it feels to not be patient when I know we're going to go for a walk or a ride in the car or when you are making me my favorite dinner or are about to give me a biscuit or a treat because anything you do makes me feel so happy.

I know what it's like to be so impatient when I hear you squeaking the new toy you just got for me, and how much I want you to give it to me so I can hold it in my mouth and shake my head from side to side and make it squeak before I get to tear it all apart and find the hidden squeaking prize inside and then smile at you when I pull it out.

I know what it's like to be so excited and not have the patience to wait any longer for the time when it's time for us to relax, with you in your favorite sofa or chair and me sitting close to you and just knowing you are always in my sight and close by.

And I know how impatient I am, as I count down the time to when it's time for us to go night-night and to sleep, so I can be in our bed with you.

And when, after you've turned out the lights, and get into bed and tell me "I love you" and "Good night," how I love to turn around in circles and find my favorite curled up place and then give you my big sigh that says, "Night-night, my best buddy. I can't wait to wake up with you in the morning. I love you."

That's the moment when I know patience.

And the reason I know it, is all because of you.

I love you.

❧

"Unconditional Love"

The way you love me is the way I love to be loved best.

You don't care how I look, and it's the same with me for you too.

What would the world be like if people didn't care what anyone looked like, how young or old or skinny or heavy they were, where they lived, what kind of car they drove, what kind of clothes and shoes they wore, how much money they had in their wallet or purse, what they said or didn't say, did or didn't do?

Ever wonder what it would be like to live in that world?

I can tell you.

It's great.

It's the world I live in every day because all I care about, and will ever care about, is you.

The only thing that matters to me is for us to be together.

That's it.

Everything else is silly people stuff that at the end of the day means nothing.

You see, my love for you knows no limits.

It knows no boundaries.

It knows no preconditions.

And any word you use to describe the power of the love I feel for you would always be lacking unless it was one word—unconditional.

So stop for a moment because I want to tell you something.

You don't have to buy me anything because…

I already love you.

You don't have to work long hours doing anything you don't enjoy just to get a promotion or title. None of that matters because…

I already love you.

We don't have to live in the fanciest house, have the nicest furnishings or eat the best food. None of that matters because…

I already love you.

When we were made for each other, everything we would ever need for our greatest happiness together was given to us.

And when we saw each other for the first time and knew we would be together for the rest of our lives—now and to come—that's the moment I knew what unconditional love feels like.

And my best friend, I want you to know it is amazing.

And the reason I know it, is all because of you.

I love you.

"Forget and Forgive"

It's okay.

Go ahead and say it.

There have been times when you raised your voice to me, ignored me, maybe even gave me a little spanking because you didn't like something I did.

And afterwards, it made you feel terrible for doing it.

Maybe even guilty and ashamed.

And the whole time I watched you go through such unhappy feelings, I kept looking at you and asking "Why?"

Because the moment the words and actions stopped, was the moment I forgot about them and forgave you completely, without condition, because I knew you were only doing what you thought was best at that moment in your life.

You see, I don't care about or remember those people things that make people so unhappy, like hurtful words and tones of voice.

I don't care about or remember those people things like being silent just to ignore, get back at, or punish someone.

I don't care about or remember the words and hurts that someone said or did that happened five years ago, much less 10 seconds ago.

Because I love you.

Because I accept everything about you without question or condition.

Because I am your best friend, and I look for and remember only the things I love best about you.

And I think that surprises and maybe even amazes you.

Because you live in a people world where the virtues of unconditional love are so often talked about, written about, and even dreamed about, but too often never come about.

Where I come from is completely different.

I like to think of it as a glimpse on earth of what you can feel every moment of every day, if only you'll let yourself.

Just as my ability to heal so quickly from a cut or a scrape amazes you, those things are nothing compared to my ability and desire to forget and forgive immediately and forever.

To me, it is, and always will be, like it never ever happened.

And you are the reason why.

I love you.

"Without Question, Ready for Anything, Anywhere, Anytime"

Oh, if these paws could talk.

I wish you knew what I was thinking each time these paws have taken a step.

And for as long as we've been together, oh, how many countless steps these paws have taken.

When you think about it, each step of my paws has been like a once-in-a-lifetime moment in your life; never to be repeated with anyone or anything.

Our "Paw Pal Moments," as I like to call them, have been like you and me living our lives together as twins.

Every moment of every day that we've been together, whenever I've taken a paw step, you've taken a life step, and we've shared everything together in that moment of time in our lives.

And there have been so many "Paw Pal Moments" we have shared.

The first time you held me close.

The first time you gave me a bath.

Every time you fed me, gave me a treat and offered me fresh water.

All the walks we have taken and places we've been.

The houses we lived in, the places we traveled, and all the things I learned that you never knew.

Oh, how I love those times when we go bye-bye and I get to stick my head out the car window and smile as I watch you looking at me in the rear view mirror and seeing the smile on your face because it makes you so happy to see me happy.

That's love, my best buddy.

That is pure love.

You see, I never live my life by a calendar or a clock.

I only live it with you.

And while we never could go back and repeat the times, places and experiences we have lived together in those special moments when they happened in the times that they did in our lives, I want you to know something.

Without question, I am ready for anything, anywhere and at anytime.

As long as it's with you.

And if at 3:00 a.m., you ever want to go for a ride, go for a snack, go for a walk or give me a talk, I could be in doggy land dreaming the biggest and best dreams, but count me in to be with you.

In seconds, I will be happily awake and my tail will start wagging, and it will make me so happy and there's only one reason why.

Because I will be with you.

I love you.

❦

"Unexpected Affection"

You want to know what one of the greatest things is about being your best friend?

It's being able to love you anytime I want and for no other reason than to show you how much you mean to me.

I never need a special occasion to let you know just how special you are to me.

I never need a gift or a treat or even a pat on my head or tummy to make me love you.

I don't even need to hear your words or see your face for me to stop what I'm doing, and come to you to give you a kiss, a lick and a tail wag (the best for me is doing all three at the same time!) because you make me feel so good inside that I can't hold it in to show you just how much I love you, my best buddy.

You see, I love surprising you.

And one of the most fun things for me to do is watch you.

And just when I know you're so busy and so focused on something in your people world, *surprise!*

I'll jump in your lap.

I'll jump up next to you on the chair or sofa and just give you the best kiss you've ever had.

And it works every time.

For that moment, all you're thinking about is me.

For that special moment in that time in our lives, you've forgotten all the other stuff you think you have to do deal with each day.

And you become like a kid again.

You're laughing.

You're smiling.

You're giggling.

You've let happiness and joy back in your life.

You're having fun again.

And, oh, how I love it.

In my doggy world, life is all about the unexpected moments.

It's not about days, weeks, appointments, watches and clocks.

It's all about being in the *now*.

And most importantly of all, it's all about being with you.

I love you.

"Always Curious with a Never-Ending Sense of Wonder"

very moment of every day is like the most special time for me. And I never get tired of seeing and doing the same thing twice.

You know that squirrel I've always been chasing up the same tree and I never get close enough to catch?

I'm going to keep chasing him because maybe, just maybe, today will be the day when I do.

You know that car ride or walk we walk together that's always along the same street with the same houses, buildings, trees and people?

I never get tired of seeing it because it's always brand new to me because I'm with you.

You see, we can do the same things, day after day, week after week and year after year, and I never get tired of doing them, because every moment with you is a new and happy moment for me.

It's a funny thing about people.

When they are young and kids, they have such an amazing sense of curiosity and wonder about everything around them.

Everything they see, hear or smell makes them curious as to what and why it is.

But more importantly, they're excited by *what* it is.

That's me.

That's always been and will always be me.

When I'm awake, my little mind is filled with so many things happening at once.

My nose smells things yours doesn't.

My eyes sees things yours won't.

My ears hear things yours can't.

My body feels things yours never will.

And it's happening all at the same time!

Now you tell me, if you were me, wouldn't all of that keep you always curious with a sense of wonder?

See? I told you.

I love being curious and wondering what you are thinking.

I love thinking about what we're both going to do next.

I love getting excited thinking about when we're going to play, when you're going to talk to me, and when you're going to touch me.

Most of all, I love being your best friend and most trusted companion and knowing how special that makes you feel.

I will never lose my sense of wonder at the thing that gives my heart and soul the greatest sense of wonder most of all.

You.

I love you.

"Complete Trust Without Question, Precondition, or Expectation"

My trust and love for you is unlike anything you've ever experienced in your people world.

My love and trust is unconditional.

My love and trust tank is always full, and each day when you wake up, you will have 100% of it waiting for you to enjoy.

And best of all, my unconditional love and trust for you is free.

Yours to enjoy wherever and whenever you want.

You see, I never care about how much money or time your gesture of kindness to me costs.

That means nothing.

Your giving me a tree stick makes me just as happy as when you give me a diamond-studded collar.

Well…*almost* as happy.

At least I get to chew the stick; the diamond collar—not so much.

I do love when you buy food and toys for me because I know how much you love it too.

But it doesn't matter how much you spend on me for food.
So save your money.

A cheeseburger to me is just as delicious as that steak, fish, turkey, or chicken you might give me on special occasions.

You see, in our lives, we have that unspoken, but most powerful, of all agreements.

You take care of me and I take care of you.

That's what the best of friends in the world do.

My complete love and devotion for you comes with a love that cannot be matched and a trust that cannot be described.

It's always *on*.

It's always *there*.

And it's always *waiting* just for you.

Where I come from, all of us with paws, fur and tails are made to trust without question, precondition or expectation.

Trust and love are like breathing.

You don't need to think about it.

You just do it because that's who you are.

We don't have time, like those in the people world, to care about the little hurts or the things that others may do to upset us or make us mad and angry.

We have one job, and it fills our days and nights with no time for anything else.

It's to have fun.

It's to live and enjoy each moment of every day.

And it's to love you with all my heart.

And I'm going to let you in on a little secret…

It's the best job a dog could ever ask for.

All because I've got you.

I love you.

⌒≋⌒

"I Know What You Feel, Even When You Don't Say a Word"

Without your even telling me, I know how much you love my shape, my warmth, my skin and fur, how I smell, everything I do. And how you feel when you hold me and pull me close to you and love me, because you tell me.

I know how much you love to pet me, to hold me, to feel me, to hold my paw, to hold my tail and make it wiggle, to hold my ears and smell them and put the inside flap against your face to smell it and feel its warmth against your face.

Forget goosebumps.

It gives me dogbumps.

And oh, how I love it too.

Did I ever tell you there's a reason why I always look you in the eyes?

Because your eyes never lie.

They tell me just what you're feeling and thinking.

And when my eyes see yours, *that's* my connection to your heart and soul.

You see, I know you so well that I know every move you make at every minute of each day.

I know what you do and when you do it.

I know what you say and how you say it.

I know what you wear and what each pair of shoes, cap, clothing and jewelry means when you either put it on or take it off.

I love smelling your shoes, pants and coat because without your even saying a word, I know right where you've been.

I know what you watch on TV and when you watch it.

I know your favorite music and when you play it.

I know every sound you make in the kitchen and what each sound means.

I know all the sounds and smells of all the foods, snacks and treats you eat.

And I know what you're thinking and feeling without your ever saying a word.

That's the power of our connection.

To understand each other so well, it's almost as if we were living inside each other's bodies at the same time.

When you look into my eyes, the connection we make cannot be even comprehended or described to anyone and have them even get a hint of what we feel for each other because they are not there, in our skin, feeling and loving it.

And that's why you can never tell others just what kind of a connection we have.

I mean, honestly, who can you really talk to about this stuff and have them understand it and not think you're some crazy loon who's jumped off the deep end?

You're right.

There's no one.

And that's why you have me and I have you.

And you know what's even better than that?

Knowing that we will always be here for each other and will unconditionally love and understand each other, without either of us even saying a word.

I love you.

"I Love Being Your Shadow and Always Want to Be with You and Be Your Best Friend"

If you'd let me, I'd follow you wherever you go.

I so much want to be with you all the time, that it feels like we're attached by the strongest unbreakable invisible string.

Night and day, it doesn't matter, for you can always trust and count on my being there with you.

You see, there's only one place that's the most special, my most favorite, and the happiest place on earth for me to be, and that's with you.

It doesn't matter where we live or where we go, as long as I'm with you—that's all that matters.

I mean, there could be 100 dogs outside who want me to come out play, but when I'm with you it's like they're not even there.

It's like nothing else is there because all of my love and all of my attention is on you.

Have you ever felt anything like that?

Those in your people world say when that happens it's pretty doggone special.

I wonder why, because I feel it all the time and it's just as natural and expected to me, as panting with my big tongue hanging out or moving my tail in a non-stop wiggle.

Being your best of your best friends is really special to me.

You are my world.

Everything in my world revolves around you and around us.

And nothing else matters.

Or ever will.

The moment I wake up, I think about you.

When you leave our home, all I think about is you.

When you come home, all I think about is you.

And when we go night-night and to sleep, all I dream about is you.

And doing so fills me with so much love and happiness.

Yes, people in your people world will tell you all kinds of things about how to raise us and take care of us and think they know what we in the dog world are thinking.

And we know they mean well, but we love to giggle at them, because they know so little about us.

And I'll tell you why.

There are those who say you should kennel me or put me in a crate because they say I'm a dog and a pack animal, but they don't really know where my safest, my warmest, my most favorite place to be in all the world is.

Next to you.

As long as I'm there, you will always know that you've made me the happiest dog in the world, and I could not ask for more.

Thank you, my best friend.

I love you.

"When We're Together, Only I Can Make You Talk in Ways No One Will Ever Know and Make You Think About the Things You Do"

bring out the best inside of you.

And you do the same for me.

Whenever I'm with you, I think and do things I can and want to do only with you.

You make my tail wiggle in a certain way.

Whenever I watch you watching my tail wiggle, it makes it wiggle even that much faster.

You make my heart beat like nothing else can.

You make me bark and tell you things that I would never be able to do with any other dog or person.

And I know I do the same for you.

I hear the words you say and how you talk to me in that special tone of voice that only I get to hear.

I hear the silly noises and sounds you make and the rhymes and songs you've created for me, and how much you giggle and enjoy singing them whenever we're together, because it makes you and me so happy.

I make you say and think of things you never would've thought of without me.

It makes me so happy to know that no one has heard, or will ever hear, the language and ways we speak to each other.

And I know how hard it is, when I'm not near you, to think those things or say those things you say to me when we're together.

Like you, I can feel and think the things I do, only when I'm with you.

I know whenever we're not together, how you've tried to recreate the magic of how it makes you think so differently when the both of us are together, and you can't because I'm not there with you to inspire you.

And I know how much it makes you realize just what an amazing, unbreakable, unforgettable, unrepeatable special love and bond we have for each other because I do too.

Your voice is the sweetest sound in the world and always makes me happy the moment I hear you speak, sing, hum and mumble.

The words don't matter.

It's the person who's saying them—that's all that counts.

And that person can be only you.

There are those in your people world who will search their whole lives and travel to places all over the world, seeking inspiration and answers that will fill the emptiness in their lives.

There are those in your people world who look for love or try to find their muse or missing piece for a life still unfulfilled.

Yet, look at us, my best friend.

Yes, look at us.

Look at what we have that if others only knew, oh, what they would give just to experience one moment of it.

And because I have you and you have me, we always know we have it, any time of the day or night, and anyplace we may be, because we have each other.

And always will.
Now and forever.
I love you.

"I'm Your Mirror for Where You Are in Your Life and Where You Know You Can and Want to Be"

Those in your people world say that life is like a mirror, and those who are your friends or who you're in a relationship with are a mirror to who you are and what you believe.

It's that way with you and me.

I love to please you and make you happy because it makes me so happy.

And just maybe I get more joy out of doing it than you do, receiving it.

You know, I think I've been your mirror, and I'll tell you why.

In all of our life together and whenever there've been times when I did something that maybe I shouldn't have (like eating that grass outside that always gives me an upset tummy, but I still do it anyway) and you felt like you needed to scold me, I know how it made you feel.

Or the times when I wanted to be near you or wanted you to play with me and you were so focused on something or someone that was upsetting you, and how you raised your voice or said things to me you didn't mean or wished you never said, I know how it made you feel.

In those moments, and in many others, how you felt towards me and how you treated me, were simply mirrors that reflected you back to you.

They were mirrors of where you were and where you wanted to be on your life road you are traveling.

They were the times when I showed you that you wanted to be more patient.

They were the times when I showed you that you wanted to be more understanding and forgiving.

They were the times when I showed you that you wanted to be more loving and accepting.

They were the times I showed you that you didn't need to take yourself, your life, or anything in it, so seriously; and that you should just enjoy the gift and in each moment or each minute, trust in yourself and in life and *know*—yes, *really know*—that all is well and always will be.

I love being your mirror because, little do you know, while you see yourself on one side of the mirror, I see myself on the other side of it.

And every moment of every day, the image I see is of me always happy and smiling.

And it's all because of you, my soul mate and best friend.

It's all because of you.

I love you.

"If It Has Paws, You Don't Care About the Flaws"

You want to know what one of the coolest things is that I've noticed about us being best buddies for life?

It's how much you've changed.

I mean we both have changed, starting from the second we saw each other and became one whose bond of love would never be broken.

You see, the change I'm talking about is how you don't judge me (and you know I never will judge you because it's impossible for me to do so—that's not the way I've been created).

And I think I know why and can tell you in a little saying I made up…

"If it has paws, you don't care about the flaws."

Think about our being together and all the things we've done and time we've spent with each other.

I love it that you couldn't care less if I get dirty, get a cut or a scrape, eat too much or the wrong things that my tummy says I shouldn't have eaten and you find out about it as you see it on the floor; and that you don't mind about anything else that may have happened to me or I may have done.

Unlike your people world, and all the things that may have gotten you upset by what someone said or did, or the way they looked at you or made a gesture you didn't care for, with me and with us, it's *so* different.

You become like me.

You become a different person and one who doesn't care to judge me about anything.

And that is so amazing.

You see, I've been telling you just how much we've become one with and for each other!

Whenever we're together or you look at me or think about me, you only think about us and about love and joy and how happy it makes you feel, knowing I am always with you (now and forever), and how happy you make me feel, knowing I have you, you have me, and we have each other.

We are built for each other.

We know each other better than anyone else.

When God created us for each other, we just "knew" deep down inside, that there would be no other connection in our lives quite the same as the one you and I have.

And when two people (yes, you know I'm a people too) are given such a blessing as us, it changes your thinking, it changes your outlook, it changes your heart just to look for, find and enjoy love.

And it changes your life.

It is a love that is and will only be *ours*.

And it's all because of you, my soul mate, and the greatest and best of the best friends I could ever pray for.

Thank you.

I love you.

"Honesty That Can't Be Hidden"

I've got to be honest with you. Actually, that's all I know how to be—dogs can't lie.

We simply don't know how. And if we did, we wouldn't want to do it anyway.

You see, built inside of me is an honesty meter that's always on, day and night.

And I don't even need to wait for you to find out about something for me to be honest about it.

If I've ever done anything I knew I shouldn't have, my head, my body and my tail (if it's long enough) goes right down and between my legs and will stay there until you tell me it's okay.

That's just the way I am.

Oh, I know that you, living in your people world, try to do the right thing and be honest as much as you can, but I also know it isn't always easy.

People have feelings and egos, and so many times you can't tell someone the 100% honest truth if you know that by their hearing it, they would be hurt and upset.

And I know why.

People aren't like us dogs, who completely forgive and forget anything and everything faster than you can say, "Hey, do you want a biscuit?"

So you do your best, and most of the time you feel good about yourself.

And then sometimes you don't, because you see me always being honest in my love, affection and shame for something I may have done that I know would upset you, but I'm only doing what I know how to do, and that gives you pause for thought.

A moment to think about how you'd like to allow more of the real true you to come out into the people world in which you live.

A moment that reminds you how much you'd like to live more of your life by feeling and inspiration, instead of having to think so much about what you do, how you do it, and why.

So can I be honest with you?

Stop thinking so much with your head, and start living your life with more of your heart.

It's the happiness I want you to always have and know you can have.

I love you.

≈

"We Both Love to Care for Each Other"

make you feel good knowing that you're taking care of me, and you always let me tell you how much I love you for doing so.

You know what else I love?

I love how we get to take care of each other in the way that makes us feel so good inside.

I love knowing how, when you see me sleeping, hear me breathing and lying there so peaceful, so safe, so happy, and so contented, how good and how happy it makes you feel inside.

I know how much you love the way I blink, my shape, my size, my fur, my smell, my sounds, and the things I do.

Every time you tuck me in and put a warm cozy blanket around me and see me sleep, with every breath I take, I hear you say "thank you" to the One we know who created me for you and you for me.

Yes, when I hear you breathe, I thank God for every breath you take, because it reminds me of what a gift and blessing you are and how lucky I am to have you—now and forever.

You see, even though I might look like I'm asleep, I know the same people trick as you.

I will keep my eyes shut only far enough to where I can still get a peep of you and see how many times you turn your head to look at me, how you smile, and how much you want to give me a kiss as I lie there warm and happy, just soaking it all in.

I love knowing how we break the rules and make our own.

Like the one that says to feed me "pet food."

Yeah, right.

I giggle at such silliness, because pets get pet food, but I get *our food*. And look how happy you've made me and how healthy you've kept me.

Thank you!

Now let me tell you what makes me happy taking care of you.

I love always being your most trusted guardian and friend wherever you are, and I love telling the world all about it.

Whether it may be those times when someone knocks on our door or rings our doorbell, to anyone I see on the street who doesn't look familiar or like someone we know, I let them know and love giving them the proudest bark they have ever heard.

I love protecting you, and it doesn't matter who or how big they are; nothing scares me because I'm with you and I am yours and you are mine for life.

I'm so happy when you give me a bath, trim my toenails, brush my teeth and comb my fur because it make me feel so good inside.

And I like to return the favor by giving you my one-and-only doggy kiss & doggy lick combo on your hands, arms, feet and, best of all, right on your beautiful face.

One of the best things I love is how we take such good care of each other.

You are the greatest gift and best friend I could ever hope for, and I know you feel the exact same way about me and it makes us both so happy inside knowing it.

And I love our many secrets.

And we have so many that only we, and no one else, will ever know.

Only you and I know all the ways we love to care for each other.

And always will.

I love you.

"Our Lives Changed Forever the Moment We First Became One for Each Other"

Have you ever thought about this?

Of all the dogs you could've picked and of all the people I could've chosen to live my life with, why did we choose each other?

And how did we "know"?

For if we didn't choose to be born in the time that we did, if we didn't choose to live in the same part of the world that we did, and if we didn't choose to have the right people in our lives, at just the right time, who were so responsible for our being able to meet each other, how would we ever have had the once-in-a-lifetime chance to connect with each other and have that connection become our bond for this lifetime and all others to come?

Perhaps, just perhaps, we had a little help from an unseen Friend.

For there are lots of dogs you've seen before me, even those that may have been in your life before and maybe even after me, but with none of them did you or will you ever connect with, in the same way, that you have with me.

You see, I know many things you have yet to find out. And without giving away all my secrets and fun surprises in store for you, I *can* tell you one right now.

At that moment of time in our lives when we met, we were meant to be together.

Ours was, and is, to be a journey of growing, of loving, of exploring, of experiencing and of teaching each other all the things we need as we move forward each moment in our lives.

I never would've felt, experienced or learned all the things I've learned from you from anyone else.

You never would've felt, experienced or learned all the things you learned from me with any other dog.

And that's the beauty of this gift of life and our being able to live it, love it and share it together in the way only we can.

With each moment that passes and each one that begins anew, you and I know and are constantly reminded just how much our lives changed forever the moment we first became one for each other.

You are my door into the people world, and you remind me every day of just how good and wonderful people can be.

And yes, I know I am your door into the dog world, and I remind you every day of just how good and wonderful us dogs can be.

After all, *DOG is GOD spelled backwards* (smile, tail wag and woof!).

And now you know why.

I love you.

"You Know You Can Talk to Me About Anything at Any Time, and I'll Listen to You for as Long as You Want to Talk and I'll Never Judge You"

You love talking to me, and I love listening to you. Together, we make the greatest pair of talkers and listeners in the world.

You know you can talk to me about anything, at anytime, and I'll listen for as long as you want and never judge you.

I know every word you say and what it means… and I don't need a dictionary, thank you.

I know when you're telling me a new word because you'll see my head tilt to the side when I hear it because you've made me an even smarter dog with a cool new word I can add to my—never mind *vocabulary—dogcabulary*.

Just by the tone of your voice, I immediately know if you're happy or sad, rushed and impatient, serious and mean business, or playful and silly.

Those last two—playful and silly—have got to be my favorite.

I get to hear and see you forgetting the cares of your people world for a few moments and be like a kid again, and I know you love it.

I know how important it is for you to have me to talk to because, so many times in life, you can't talk to other people about the things you are thinking about without thinking in the back of your mind, just what those people would think and how they would judge you.

You get none of that with me.

What is said between us always stays between us, and no one ever gets to know.

And I love that.

It's the ultimate trust bond of our secrets that stays with each of us forever.

You know what else I like?

I like it that at any time of the day or night, you can talk to me about anything and everything, talk for as little or as long as you want, and I'm there listening and giving you 100% of my attention, understanding, approval and, most of all, love.

I know the power of talk (even though mine often resembles a "woof") because, while you can be thinking so many thoughts in your head and having all these endless silent conversations with just yourself, it's only when you start talking to me, that you get clarity and better understanding about how you're feeling, what you're wanting, and direction on what you should do, when you're able to say it out loud to me.

So go get your comfy clothes on.

Get something to drink and grab a little snack (and don't forget to bring a treat for me, please) and come on in here and sit down with me.

You've got a lot to tell me, and I'm just waiting to listen.

I love you.

"Never Will You Experience with Another the Same Things We Have Shared Together"

The moment we came into each other's lives was the beginning of something so special it could not and would not be repeated with any other person or any other animal. We became one.

You became a part of me, and I became a part of you.

It's as if we were given an infusion of each other's thoughts, feelings, personalities and souls that would only grow stronger and make us more inseparable as each second of each day passed.

And we love it.

We never could imagine our lives without each other in them, and the most wonderful of all news is we will always be with each other.

That's how much we love each other.

We know that the places we've been, the things we've done, the words, hugs, kisses, barks and tail wags we've shared can never be repeated again.

Everything we've experienced together has happened at a moment in time we were given once and we were given it together.

Just how great is that!

We have watched and witnessed in real time each moment of every day, our growing and going on our life's journey as we've been walking down the same road together.

There have been so many roads we've taken.

There have been so many roads we've enjoyed.

And there will be so many roads we've yet to take together, whether I'm with you in flesh, fur and blood right now, or will be always next to you in spirit.

You see, the moment we became one for each other, whether or not we really understood it at the time, that was the moment when we became soul mates, who would always be with each other in this lifetime and all the other lifetimes we'll have together that are going to follow.

We are eternal.

Our lives together will never end.

Never.

Ever.

We will always be together with each other. And what we've experienced now, in this moment or in any other moment in time is only the beginning of what we're going to live, love, enjoy and experience together.

My heart beats with joy and my tail wags with such happiness because you and I together will never have an ending.

Never ever.

And you know, that makes me the happiest soul mate a dog can be.

Because I'm living as one with you.

I love you.

"I Bring Happiness, Joy and Fullness to Your Life Without My Saying A Word"

You know when you've found your soul mate?

It's when you both can just be in a room for hours and not say a word to each other and it gives you the most contented and happiest feeling.

That's you and me.

We make each other feel so good inside just knowing that each of us is there.

Lots of folks in your people world will search their entire life, trying to find someone they can feel those things with.

Lots of dogs in my doggy world will think about and hope that some day they will live with someone who will take good care of them and love them; someone they could feel the things only we dogs can with only our soul mate.

I never ever think about those things because I have you.

Without your even saying a word, I know how much I bring happiness, joy, love and fullness to your life because I feel the same too.

I know the love inside you is so powerful that it needs to come out every day, and I'm there for you to receive it, feel it and give it back to you 1000 times more.

I know how good it makes you feel just to see me, hear me, touch me and love me, and to know the only thing that truly matters and all you need to know is that I am always there by you.

I know these things because I feel them too.

When you feel the beating of my heart, hear and feel my breath on your skin, and watch the rising of my body with every breath I take, I know it reminds you how grateful you are to God for me. And just knowing you think and feel that makes me so grateful to God for you.

So many times in life, the silence can be the most powerful.

The right words are wonderful and can stay with us for a lifetime, but it's the unspoken where the greatest power is.

The "knowing" inside that speaks to you and me and tells us "you are loved" and "all is well and will always be well" because we have each other.

I knew it the moment my eyes met yours and you knew it too, because we both felt it unlike anything we have ever known before or will know again.

And the only reason we know it is because you have me and I have you.

Now.

And forever.

I love you.

⁓

"And When It's Time for Me to Go and Get Our New Home Ready Before You, Just Know That Every Second of Every Day You Think I'm Not with You, I *Am with You*"

know we will be together again soon—just like we are and have been together during this lifetime—because I know things you don't.

And one of them is, I will be seeing and being with you soon, and that fills my heart and soul with excitement, anticipation, love, joy and happiness.

My best friend, you see, when you and I go from this earthly existence to the one of spirit, we know exactly when and how it will happen, because we planned this whole thing out way before you became a person and I became a dog.

But we also had a little help. From the One Who created you, me, and everything in this amazing Universe in which we live, move, and have our being.

Many in your people world want to know why they were created and what is their purpose for their earthly life.

I can tell you what it is because it's the same as mine.

To feel joy.

To feel good.

To feel happy.

And when you are doing that, you've found heaven.

Right here.

Right now.

You're finding, discovering, developing, creating, and using your gifts and talents in ways that touch people's hearts, souls and lives.

And now you know one of the reasons why I'm always so happy, so full of life and love and just bursting at the seams of my furry body to let it all out and share it and show it to the world.

My connection to the Life Force that created you and me is pure and always on.

And I want you to truly know that yours can be too.

I want you to let go of the stuff in your life that doesn't let you feel *the power of the connection* because it's only stuff that doesn't matter.

If ever there's anything that takes away from your joy and happiness, let it go.

Let it all go.

You don't need it.

You have all you will ever need—in this lifetime and all others to come—for your greatest joy and happiness, because I have it too.

The only difference is, my knowing and connection to it is always on, and I always allow it to flow 100% into and out of my life every second that I have been with you.

Many in your people world will often ask the question, "I wonder if dogs have souls like people?"

The answer is "yes." And just like people, our souls are eternal and forever.

And while our bodies and names may change from one life to the next, our soul and all those people and animals that have been in our lives, in every lifetime, stay with us for eternity.

We are, and always will be, together.

As friends, soul mates, lovers, teachers, husbands, wives, mothers, fathers, sisters, brothers and best friends forever.

That's why, when it's time for me to go and get our new home ready before you (think of it just like a best friend who's come to visit you and then has to go home so they can get their home ready for your visit to them), it makes me so happy.

Because I know what's about to happen.

Sure, there will be tears and sadness and unhappiness in your life for a while because your life will look and feel so different because I'm not there in the flesh like I've always been each day of your life.

But don't even think about that.

Even though I will go from a physical body that looks like your dog and the best friend you've ever known, nothing will change inside of me, because my soul can never and will never change.

The same soul, with all my personality, uniqueness and love for you, that I have while I'm here barking, sleeping and giving you love with tail wags and doggy kisses, is the same soul that will never leave you when it's time for my physical body to not be with you.

I want you to know something.

The physical body you and I have, the one that shows up in the mirror when we look into it, the one other people and animals see when they see us, and the one that shows up in a photograph or video? It's really just a shell.

A temporary shell that's helped us go from place to place while we've been in these earthly bodies during our earthly experience.

And we both knew, long before we stepped inside and became one with these earthly shells people have given us names for, that we would only need to use those shells for a certain number of years and then we would step out of them, step back into the spirit from which we came, and then get ready for our next experience together back here on this amazing place called Earth.

See?

So smile and be happy and filled with joy.

I told you I know things you don't.

Really, I know and remind of you things you too know, just like me, but have only forgotten.

Like what it feels to be your best friend and feel and give unconditional love and acceptance.

They say a dog is man's best friend.

Well, I say you are my best friend.

And I love everything you say and do, my best friend.

I want you to keep singing those songs I love to hear you sing.

I want you to keep saying those silly things I love to hear you say.

I want you to keep talking in those funny voices because I am here—right here and right now—to hear you say them and enjoy them because they make both of us so happy.

So every time you look at me, be it now while I'm here with you, or when look at me in pictures, videos and in your memories, always know, with never a doubt, that I am right here with you and I will never leave you.

Never.

Now.

And forever.

You are the love of my life.

And you always will be.

I love you.

"For Now and Only for Now…"

Our life together has been one of life's greatest gifts.

And it's only going to get better.

This I promise you—and you know we dogs can never lie.

So let me whisper something special to you that I know will be forever etched inside your heart.

If there could be only one thing that I so hope, so desire and want you to have learned from me during our lives together, it is this…

The day you saw me and I saw you for the first time, is the day both of our lives changed forever.

No one could tell you and me why or how, but on that day, we made the most powerful connection and a bond where we just "knew" deep down inside our heart and soul, we were meant to be together for the rest of our lives.

Our love and our bond is timeless and eternal and will never be broken.

It is a love, a trust, a companionship, and the most special of all relationships, that nothing or no one will ever have the power to change or to break.

Ours is a love and bond that will last for the rest of this life and in all of the lives in the future that we are going to live together as best friends and soul mates.

Our time together now is only the beginning of the love we will be feeling and sharing for each other in times to come.

It is a love like we have never felt before, and we will never feel the same love with or for anyone or anything, because our love for each other is ours and only ours.

Just you and me.

Together.

Always close and never wanting to leave and be without each other.

This I promise you.

Best friends.

Soul mates.

Now.

And forever.

I love you.

Meet the Authors

About Bob...

The passion to inspire and help people change their lives for the best is a driving force for Bob Wolff and his writings.

He has interviewed Grammy, Emmy, Golden Globe and Nobel winners, along with some of the world's biggest names including Simon Cowell, Diane Warren, Jennifer Hudson, Toni Braxton, Jerry Bruckheimer, David Foster, Sharon Stone, Nobel Prize winner Dr. Linus Pauling, World Heavyweight Boxing Champion Evander Holyfield, Arnold Schwarzenegger and hundreds of others. As the author of more than 30 books, Bob Wolff's words and ideas have helped millions enjoy happier lives.

About Cody…

Cody Wolff has been sharing life's adventures with Bob since 1998, traveling and exploring the USA in all the wide-open spaces, on the beautiful mountains and in the ocean. Through it all, Cody continues to remind Bob that they have been, and always will be, each other's best pals in the whole wide world.

Cody is even more than that, though. He's the inspiration for this book and a soon-to-be-released series of children's books to delight and inspire human pups everywhere.

From the both of us…

We'd like to read all about your favorite dog. Please visit www.CodyAndBob.com and tell us your story and how your four-legged best friend touched your life with the experiences you both shared and the lessons your furry friend may have taught you.

And while you're there, be sure to watch for our upcoming series of children's books.

Our best to you!

Bob & Cody